THE WOBBLE

Teen, Pregnant, and Courageous

Yani Alfonso, Ed.S.

Tandem Light Books

THE WOBBLE: Teen, Pregnant, and Courageous

Copyright © 2020 Yani Alfonso

ISBN: 978-1-7351959-1-9

What Readers are Saying —

Praise for, *The Wobble: Teen, Pregnant, and Courageous*

"Excellent read!!! *The Wobble* is a wonderfully deep story of which all teens should be able to relate. You are immediately drawn in through visualizing the perseverance and tenacity it took to walk off the bus at the beginning of the story. It is easy to foresee how students will be able to connect to the character's steadfast ability to wobble off the bus as a representation of any experiences of adversity. We all have growing pains, no matter how large or small, and this story is able to capture how difficult it is to walk through life-changing events and see something great on the other side." – **Ashley Martin, M.S. – Teacher**

"Being a teen can be challenging within itself because of all the peer pressure that comes along with it, especially when all eyes are focused on you. "The Wobble" is a roller coaster of raw emotions when the unexpected happens, and at the same time it is a story of triumph and encouragement for the reader." - **Marjorie Gettys - Author**

"Encouraging, inspirational - a story of a young lady who had the courage to keep doing what needed to be done in order to achieve her long-term goal, no matter how difficult. It is the story of the joy of accomplishment, even with pain along the way." - **Dr. Marilyn Mahabee-Harris – Clinical Psychologist**

"Wobble shares the amazing story and lesson that young women can achieve their dreams while working through incredibly difficult challenges such as pregnancies and tragedies. It encourages self-worth, perseverance, and strength." - **Zaira D. Solano, Esq. – Attorney**

"A brave, strong character and a writing style that evokes a deep sense of empathy. Yani writes such elegant and practical prose as she develops her character in a way that the reader feels like they are walking in her shoes on the very first page! The engaging, meticulous illustrations combined with the readable fashion of writing, make this a relevant read for preteens and teens. This novel should be in every school media center in the country." - **Kamaria Muhammad – Teacher**

More Praise for,

The Wobble: Teen, Pregnant, and Courageous

"Wobble embodies the rawness that is often hidden from young people, despite their constant need for open conversation. Alfonso meets teens where they are with a story that takes courage to tell but one that leaves readers with an understanding of teen pregnancy that is like no other." - **Amanda Triplett, Ed.S - Teacher**

"The Wobble: A powerful, short, sweet, and very intimate story that leaves you feeling hopeful and motivated to face any experience life throws at you with love, faith, and your head held up high. What does not break you can only make you stronger. The sky is the limit!" - **Angélica G. Negron, LCSW, RPT-S – Social Worker**

"A beautiful and empowering story of teen pregnancy. This book provides hope and support to those on this journey. Inspiring and encouraging to read. I look forward to the next one." - **Tracey Wooten – Social Worker**

Free Gift

JUST FOR TEENS

JUST FOR TEACHERS

JUST FOR PARENTS

Go to: http://eepurl.com/g_8_PL

All proceeds from this non-profit book will benefit children, parents, teachers, and low-income families through the outreach of Tandem Life Books.

Tandem Life Books:

educate, inspire, live better

DEDICATION

To my husband,

Guely,

my tandem life partner, best friend &

wind beneath my wings.

FOREWORD

My first encounter with Yanira Alfonso was on the day that I took my oldest child to meet his new teacher at his new school, where she, in turn, was learning all about her new school for the first time after moving to a new state. She gave the impression of being confident in her ability to handle all the new situations that were certainly going to transpire, as well as exuding a sense of fun that would be necessary to gain the love and trust of her classroom of active first graders. I still remember and have the little booklet she made with a picture of each child in her class for the parents to have from their first day – a truly special and unexpected gift that captured the essence of the person she was and has continued to be.

The Wobble is a book written from her personal experience with the difficulty that it takes to allow oneself to deliberately move forward and do something that will require intense emotional stress. It also lets the reader know that it is normal to have a lot of negative thoughts come into your head and that it can be hard to resist those ideas. The reader will easily capture the feelings both from the text and the graphic designs, and this encourages perusal of the entire story to see what happens. It is a story of a young lady who had the courage to keep doing what needed to be done in order to achieve her long-term goal, no matter how difficult. It is the story of the joy of accomplishment, even with pain along the way.

Mrs. Alfonso has generously let the reader know that she welcomes feedback at the end of her book and encourages suggestions for topics that would be of interest for future books. The Wobble focuses on a topic that is difficult to bring up in general conversation with young people. This book now provides a wonderful way to introduce the concept that even people who have been successful in life, have not always gotten there without difficult situations that they did not anticipate having to overcome. I recommend this as a story that can be used for small group discussions, as a writing prompt for young people to share their thoughts, and as a book to simply think about for oneself. Hopefully, all who read it will find a message that encourages as well as inspires.

Marilyn Mahabee-Harris, PhD

Clinical Psychologist

The heat was at its peak the summer after my high school junior year. It was that same summer that I wobbled off the big yellow school bus seven months pregnant. The kids froze as if at once, turning in unison, eyes bulging first at my face and then at my very pregnant belly.

I picked up my head, fought my way through the crowd, and walked straight to the classroom, determined to retake my social studies final.

I felt my face grow hot, and sweat roll

down my protruding belly. I collapsed

into the chair. My stomach

popped out sideways. It had

wedged itself between the back of

the chair and the fixed arm table that

was part of the desk.

As if needing to escape, I instantly drifted back to simpler days.

Although I don't quite remember the boy's name, I remember exactly how he made me feel. His hand shot up! "Ooh! Teacher, me! Teacher, pick me!" "Okay, what did you get for Christmas?" asked our second-grade teacher.

I think what he said was that he got a

Dune Buggy, Punch Me Toy, Silly

Putty, GI Joe, an astronaut, clothes, a

pair of Pro-Ked sneakers, train, Hot

Wheels, tracks, lots of cars to go with

them, and, and...

I rolled my eyes, and my mouth dropped as I heard him boast about yet another toy on his long list! "Naaa, that's not possible," I thought, but he kept rambling.

As his list grew longer, my heart sank lower and lower.

My body slumped deeper and deeper into my chair as each student was called upon.

I was absolutely horrified about letting anyone know that I only received one gift!

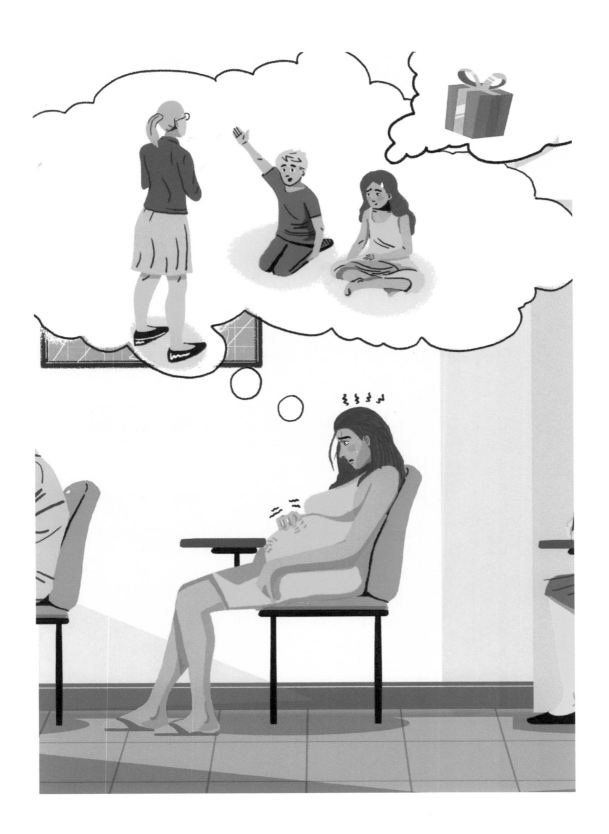

My heart started to beat faster and faster, and my hands were drenched in sweat. With each, "Thump! Thump," I rubbed them on my dress while at the same time trying to catch my breath.

My lip began to quiver, and my left eye began to twitch. I was a mess! An uncontrollable mess!

How desperately I imagined myself becoming a flat figure that could discretely slip all the way down to the floor, slither unnoticed under the desks, under the cabinets, slipping under the classroom door, and into the hallway.

Then, **popping** itself back into shape and making a run for it, right out of the school building!

I snapped back to reality when my blurred vision

zoomed into focus, clearly noticing

the very pregnant belly and the exam sitting on my

desk. Here I sat in this chair feeling the very same way

as that day when I was only eight. "If I go to the

bathroom, I can miss this test altogether, but what

good would that do?"

 I would never find out if I failed or succeeded. I would

never find out if wobbling down the big yellow school

bus was worth it. I had to try. I had to give it my best. I

knew this was something I would not regret.

As my fingers met the test paper that inevitably held

my future, my hands got clammier, and my eyes could

not come to rest. My eyes fidgeted and fidgeted!

"Focus! Focus!"

Then, my dad's words rung in my ears, "School is

important! School is your ticket out of poverty. Give it

all you have, so that you don't have to work as hard as

I have had to work."

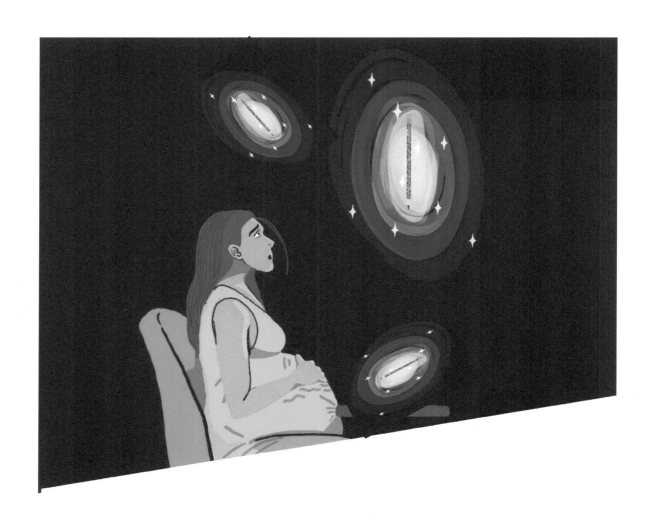

Magically, the pencil fell into my hand.

To my heart's delight, the test questions were the questions I had just reviewed on the break. I wrote, and I wrote.

I didn't stop until it was all done!

Minutes became hours, and hours

became days, until the day I found out,

that I passed the test!

It was a C. I didn't regret it. The

wobble was worth it!

Months later, not wobbling or doubting, regretting, or fretting, I would **proudly** march to get another piece of paper, one that would open up doors to more education, one that would make me feel proud without hesitation.

It was at that moment in time that I learned the wobble would no longer define me. Ongoing daily stares would no longer haunt me and hurt me. I was **stronger, braver**, and full of hope for a brighter future, not only for me but also for my baby, which I held in one arm while also holding the Parchment High School diploma paper.

STRONGER!

BRAVER!

PROUD!

Although I wish I could say that the

role of mom was a new role for me, it

was not the case.

It was I who took care of my little

brother and sister. You see, my dad

had tragically passed away.

I was the first in my family to

graduate from high school, and the

impact was such that I was not the

last.

The July heat, the sweat, and the

suffering of that wobble, when I

first got off the big yellow school

bus, was definitely worth it!

Epilogue

The Wobble: Teen, Pregnant, and Courageous is based on the real-life events of Yanira Alfonso. Twelve years after her high school graduation, while taking one to two evening classes at a time, juggling children, school, and family, Yani honored her father's memory and desire for her to "become a professional." She graduated with her Bachelor's Degree in Education. Later on, she obtained her Master's Degree in Teaching Additional Languages, and finally, she proudly marched for the last time to receive her Education Specialist Degree in Curriculum and Instruction.

At the time of this publication, Yani and her childhood friend and high school sweetheart have been married over 41 years. Their two grown children, both educated professionals, have made them proud, and their three grandchildren have surpassed the expectations of what it means to bring joy. Yani calls her husband, Miguel, her tandem partner not only because they enjoy cycling on a tandem bike but because he has always been her ultimate support. Had it not been for him and her faith, this story would have a very different ending.

Yani and Guely

June, 1980 - High School Graduation

July 12, 1992 – Bachelor's Degree

August 4, 2001 – Master's Degree

May 5, 2007 – Education Specialist Degree

Afterword

Yani Alfonso, Ed.S.

Did you know that:

1. In 2017, a total of 194,377 babies were born to women 15-19 years of age (Hamilton, JA, Hamilton, BE., & Osterman, MJK, 2017).

2. The U.S. teen pregnancy rate is substantially higher than in other western industrialized nations (Sedgh, G., Finer, LB., Bankole, A., Eilers, MA., & Singh S, 2015).

3. Racial/ethnic and geographic disparities in teen birth rates persist, both within and across states (Romero, L., Pazol, K., Warner, L., et al., 2006-2007, 2013-2014).

When I first shared the cover of this book, *The Wobble: Teen, Pregnant, and Courageous,* on social media, I was accused by one individual of being part of "the problem" encouraging "this type of behavior" because I was writing about teen pregnancy. His comment only affirmed how much I needed to write this book. An unplanned teenage pregnancy, for many young women, is a traumatizing, painful experience, complicated by an array of life circumstances, childhood experiences, past hurts, and sometimes psychological issues. Only someone who has experienced that immense pain can empathize with those impacted by teen pregnancy.

The problem is that often women who choose to speak about the teen pregnancy topic suffer judgments all over again, awakening old wounds; therefore, for many women, it is easier to keep silent. Years ago, the comment from the gentleman on social media would have stopped me from sharing my story, but I am thankful for the strength that has emerged out of healing. It has taken over forty years of much-needed self-forgiveness for me to be able to pen the words of this book. Truly, nothing is impossible. I chose to open myself up to criticism and judgment by writing this book because I don't want it to take forty years for others to find that same strength. Life is too short. We should live each day to the fullest.

I chose to write a graphic novel because pictures speak a universal language. As a teacher, I also wanted this topic to be accessible to all readers. It was not my intent for the short graphic novel to answer all of "the questions," but instead, its purpose was to provoke the reader to raise questions and ignite passionate conversations. Hopefully, along the way, it will also encourage every person to engage in a discussion about topics that might make him or her uncomfortable.

Teen pregnancy may seem to be the end of the world, as it appeared once for me, but the theme of this book is that no matter how difficult things may get, it is not the end of the world. Your mistakes do not have to write your destiny nor map out your future. You can do more than survive; you can thrive! You can heal! You can still succeed! You can have internal peace and experience joy and happiness! Who knows? One day, you will inspire and help someone else.

If, after reading this graphic novel, you have questions that I did not answer, I invite you to email me your questions at yani@tandemlifebooks.com. I desire very much to meet the hero in you. Please share your story. Also, please let me know about the things you wish I would include in future books. As a gift for you, I have three free resources that you may download for you, a friend, a parent, or a teacher.

For your gift go to: http://eepurl.com/g_8_PL

Remember what I mentioned earlier about feeling judged? Well, what if I told you my most intimate secret? What if I told you the secret that would evaporate and dissipate most of those judgments or raise new ones? What if I told you the secret that every teen should know, needs to know, but no one ever tells them? For that, you will have to read my next book: *"But I Didn't…Teen, Pregnant, and Shocked."*

Sign up at: https://tandemlifebooks.com/the-wobble-teen-pregnant-and-courageous to be entered into a drawing for a free copy of the next book. If you enjoyed this book, please recommend it to a friend and write a review. I would love to know what you thought of it. Please contact me if you would like me to speak with your youth group or women's group.

I look forward to hearing from you.

Until next time,

Yani

Yani@tandemlifebooks.com

Postscript

My dad died tragically on Christmas Eve, December 24, 1979, three months after he met his first grandbaby. I hold his memory forever.

"Dad, thanks for your love and inspiration. Your memory kept me going on days when I thought I would not make it. I love you, dad."

After my dad's death, it was this precious baby that gave me the courage to get up each morning. It was an unbelievable high school senior year! God used a negative situation to save my life. My new baby gave me purpose and a reason to push forward and thrive. In our darkness, it is difficult to see the big picture, but God sees it. One day, I may share that part of my story. "Thank you, my sweet girl."

Summer 1979, when Yani walked off that big yellow school bus.

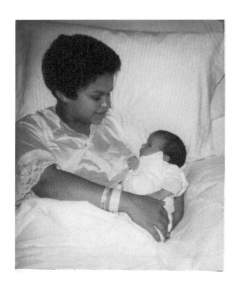

September 1979, Yani and her five days old baby.

Acknowledgments

Miguel Alfonso – We were children raising children. We have grown up together. Thank you, honey, for always being my great supporter, my tandem partner, for the many hours you took care of our two children so that I could go to classes and study, for the many hours you have arduously worked to always provide for our family, and for the many diapers you changed to make it happen for us. You are an amazing example of what it means to be a real man, one who hangs in there in good times and in bad times, in sickness and in health. I am privileged to have shared over 41 years of marriage with you. Thank you! I love you!

Annette and Miguel, Jr. Alfonso – I am blessed to have the most incredible children in the world. Thank you, Annette and Guelito, for your love, help, understanding, and support the MANY years that mom juggled home, school, and family. Thanks for encouraging me to write this book. I love you! You both make me so proud!

Xiomara and Roberto Caraballo – My dear brother and sister, we share a history and a special bond as siblings. I am proud of both of you. **Xiomy**, your humble, loving heart is admirable. What would I have done without you those first years of me being a teen mom? I can't even imagine. Thank you for the many hours of babysitting, love, encouragement, and support. I love you, my Sis!

Dona Toña – Thanks Dona Toña for taking care of my children while I went to school during the summers. I still remember the day when I marched through the congratulations line with my Bachelor's Degree in hand. My eyes met yours. They spoke about the twelve years that it took me to complete that college degree, but they communicated so much more. You are gone, but that moment in time is forever engraved in my memory and my heart. Thank you for being there for my family and me.

Grasi Suarez – Mom, thanks for accepting Jesus into your life and being a changed woman, whom I love more now than when I was a child. Our relationship is evidence of how God can mend wounds, empower us to forgive, and love again. God is truly in the miracle business. Thank you, mom. I love you.

Mrs. Holland, Mrs. Hoyer, Mrs. Doherty, Mrs. Cummings, and "that teacher" – I want to thank these teachers who stand out in my mind. They are real educators who shaped and made me into the person I am today. They represent the many teachers that genuinely care for their students and go above and beyond to make sure their students are learning in a meaningful, fun way while keeping them safe.

Family and Friends – If you offered a word of encouragement or said a prayer for me, along life's way, I want to thank you. We need each other. It is difficult to do life alone. Thank you.

Finally, many made direct contributions to the publishing of this book. Thank you!

Blurbs -

I am grateful to all those who took the time out of their busy schedules to read *The Wobble: Teen, Pregnant, and Courageous* and write a blurb.

Teachers:

Candy DeBolt, Ed.S.

Pam Eichberg, Ed.S.

Ashley Martin, M.S.

Kamaria Muhammad

Jeannie Potter

Amanda Triplett, Ed.S.

Cristina Zakis

Authors:

Dr. Katherine Arnoldi, author of the book, *The Amazing "True" Story of a Teenage Single Mom.*

Marjorie Gettys, author of the book, *God's Clouds and Umbrellas.*

Zaira Solano, **Esq.**, author of the book, *Alpha Couples: Build a Powerful Marriage Like a Boss.*

Psychologist and Social Workers:

Marilyn Mahabee-Harris, PhD

Angélica G. Negron, LCSW, RPT-S

Tracey Wooten

Katherine Arnoldi, PhD - I am honored and very grateful to **Dr. Katherine Arnoldi** for taking time to read my graphic novel and provide valuable feedback. Dr. Arnoldi is the author of the graphic novel, *The Amazing "True" Story of a Teenage Single Mom,* which I highly recommend. She is a Fulbright Fellow (2008-2009) and has been awarded two New York Foundation of the Arts Awards (Fiction and Drawing), a Newhouse Award, The Henfield Transatlantic Fiction Award, and the Dejur Award. After reading Dr. Arnoldi's graphic novel, *The Amazing "True" Story of a Teenage Single Mom,* and finding out that she is an advocate for equal rights to education for single moms, I knew I had to attempt to connect with her. It would be a dream come true for me. I am humbled and touched by your response, Dr. Arnoldi. Thank you.

Foreword: Thank you, **Dr. Marilyn Mahabee-Harris**, for your immense love for children and families all of your life and for all that you do in your profession. You are an exceptional person. I am honored that you took time out of your busy schedule to write the foreword of this book. Thank you.

Editing and revising: **Annette and Adam Heck, Xiomara Caraballo, Amanda Triplett, and Mitch Doxsee** for reminding me that I had a story to tell.

Graphic Designer/Illustrations: Vishal Kadian @illust.artist

Photography – author pictures: **Annette Heck** Photography

https://www.facebook.com/annetteheckphotography/

https://www.instagram.com/annetteheckphotography/

Social Media Advice: Robert and Zaira Solano (Authors of the book, *Alpha Couples: Build a Powerful Marriage Like a Boss*).

Finally, I want to thank my childhood babysitter, **Doña Aura**, for introducing me to prayer. I would not have made it through the tough times in my life without my Heavenly Father and my faith. Her memory will always live in my heart. She gave me the greatest gift.

Questions: yani@tandemlifebooks.com.

Free Gift: http://eepurl.com/g_8_PL

Free Book: drawing, "*But I Didn't…Teen, Pregnant, and Shocked,*" at https://tandemlifebooks.com/the-wobble-teen-pregnant-and-courageous.

Your Review Appreciated: If you enjoyed this book, I appreciate it if you take the time to write a review and recommend it to a friend.

Please contact me if you would like me to speak with your youth group or women's group. It has been a remarkable journey!

Until next time,

Yani,

yani@tandemlifebooks.com

About the Author

Yani Alfonso, Ed.S.

Yani Alfonso enjoys teaching English Language Learners in her middle school Literacy Connections classes. She holds a Bachelor's Degree in Education, a Master's Degree in Teaching Additional Languages, and an Ed.S. Degree in Curriculum and Instruction. Her experience includes district trainer, instructional coach, conference speaker, K-8 content and ESOL teacher (English to Speakers of Other Languages).

 Her husband of 41+ years has been her tandem partner in all of her endeavors. He was an anchor early in their marriage when she was a student, teen mom, and wife. They have been blessed with two loving, very well accomplished grown children and three grandchildren. Yani's life is an example of what it means to come out on the other side of poverty, pain, and turmoil and succeed despite life's circumstances.

"Somewhere along the path of life, we must all find a way to step out of our comfort zone, choose others before self, to support and help someone else. *The Wobble: Teen, Pregnant, and Courageous* is my step out of my comfort zone to support others and inspire them along the way" – ya.

Final Praise for,

The Wobble: Teen, Pregnant, and Courageous

"Inspiring others, Yanira Alfonso tells her story here of being a teenage mother in high school and how she, despite her obvious pregnancy and despite being bullied, insisted on her right to equal access to education."- **Dr. Katherine Arnoldi -Author**

"Yani's passion for children and family is evident in *The Wobble*. It was heartfelt, and you could feel the passion she had for her baby. I loved the Graphic Novel format for teens. My hope is that this book will help other teens in the same situation." - **Pamela Eichberg, Ed.S – Teacher**

"Yani has created a blessing for many through this beautiful sharing of her story. In this simple yet deeply inspiring retelling, she has shared some of her strength and courage with young women facing a similar challenge, to move forward and reach for a goal despite what may be perceived as a setback. She overcame her fears to provide a life for her baby, herself, and her future family. I am blessed by Yani's example. What a great book to share with teen moms and their friends and families. It's a story of hope!" - **Cristina Zakis -Teacher**

"Wobble gives the reader a glimpse into the struggles Yani overcame through faith, determination, and hard work to be a successful educator and writer. An excellent read for any teenager, but especially those in need of encouragement so they too can overcome the challenges they face." - **Candy DeBolt, Ed.S. – Teacher**

"So many young girls go through the experience of teen pregnancy alone, isolated and ashamed. The message of THE WOBBLE is one of hope and joy for many young teens! Thank you for sharing your experience in such a unique way. This is sure to have a positive impact on many young women!" - **Jeannie Potter – Teacher**

References

Hamilton, JA., Hamilton, BE., & Osterman, MJK. (2017). NCHS data

brief 2018. *Births in the United States*, (319):1-8.

Romero, L., Pazol, K., Warner, L., et al. (2006-2007, 2013-2014, 2016).

MMWR Morbidity and mortality weekly report. *Reduced*

Disparities in Birth Rates Among Teens Aged 15-19 Years –

United States, 65(16):409-414.

Sedgh, G., Finer, LB., Bankole, A., Eilers, MA., & Singh S. (2015).

Adolescent Health. *Adolescent pregnancy, birth, and abortion*

rates across countries: levels and recent trends, 56(2):223-30.

Thank you for your support of the educational outreach of Tandem Life Books. All proceeds from this non-profit book will benefit children, parents, teachers, and low-income families.

Tandem Life Books: educate, inspire, live better

Lightning Source UK Ltd.
Milton Keynes UK
UKHW050837141220
375018UK00003B/56